Control and Survive a Police Stop

Don't Get Shot Know What to Do

Tony Walker
7/9/2016

Control and Survive a Police Stop,

Don't Get Shot Know What to Do

COPYRIGHT © 2016 TONY WALKER, BE SAFE LIVING

ALL RIGHTS RESERVED.

Published by Kindle Direct Publishing

ISBN9781536959062

Contents

PREFACE i
INTRODUCTION v
UNDERSTANDING THE OFFICER 1
STATISTICS 5
REASONABLE SUSPICION 7
    Profiling 14
ENCOUNTERS 15
SEARCHES 19
    Consent Searches 21
    Body Searches Pat Downs/Frisk 26
OBSERVATIONS 31
    Mistake of Fact 33
WHEN DETAINED 36
    Concealed Weapon Permit 39
    Traffic Stops 41
    The DUI Stop 45
ORDERS to STAND BACK 51
    Recording 53
    Use of Recordings 56
    Public Disclosure 57
    Domestic Disturbance 57
WARRANTS 59

    Interrogations 63
    The Arraignment 67
    Unlawful Arrest 72
RULES OF EVIDENCE 75
CORRUPTION 77
COMPLAINTS 81
PRIVATE SECURITY 85
    CONCLUSION 87

PREFACE

Most citizens view a police officer as responsible for protecting and serving the community. They see police encounters after a (911) call or a law violation. Parents, family, and friends usually teach children to communicate with law enforcement. Inappropriate behavior with the police can lead to things going wrong. There are communities where a routine police encounter can lead to death.

I am a 69-year-old African American male, a retired Correctional Lieutenant, who worked over twenty-eight years in the California Correctional system. I know how to respond when interacting with law enforcement. However, my encounters with law enforcement are high compared to the average citizen; the police have stopped me over twelve times. My encounters differ in many ways from the rest of the population.

One encounter occurred in an airport as I exited the airplane. A plainclothes officer stopped me without identifying himself and asked for my ID. His partner stood behind me less than a foot away. Knowing what his partner would do, my experience influenced my decision to give him my ID without question. After realizing my status as a retired officer, he gave my ID back to me and said thank you. I asked why he stopped me; he showed me a photo and said he was "looking for someone." The only thing I had in common with his suspect was we were bald.

On two occasions, officers directed me out of my car, and no reason was given as they drew their weapons. During one stop, I turned a corner and passed a police car; as they were parked, they pulled out and followed me to my home, where they drew their weapons on me. Once I identified as an officer and they saw my ID, they retreated to their vehicles. Before they left, I asked why they stopped me; they stated we "heard you speeding." I did not report or complain about the stops.

My career and experience have led me to hold a false belief that law-abiding citizens should not fear the police. Some encounters with law enforcement are scary and filled with fear. Being armed and stopped by an officer causes me a degree of terror (will the officer respond to my having a concealed weapon before I can explain?

Researching police stops to see if my contacts were average, and I surveyed friends and acquaintances of all ethnic backgrounds and genders. I discovered that my Black male friends were stopped about six to eight times in their lives. My white male friends had been stopped about three times. Most people I questioned were over the age of fifty.

Government databases did not provide information on the number of stops the average citizen makes or statistics on common encounters. Law enforcement contacts are minor compared to the number of law violations. Police can make a traffic stop every fifteen minutes because many citizens are unaware they are violating a traffic law.

The percentage of encounters increases based on gender and race. Controlling these encounters is a matter of attitude. The person in control is the person with the power to influence and direct the thoughts and movements of others. The person who establishes respect, a sense of fear, or empathy controls the other person.

This book is not an attempt to teach the law but a guide to interactions with law enforcement to survive and exit the encounter without being harmed or going to jail.

INTRODUCTION

The police should establish rapport; citizens should not have to deal with a difficult officer. One way to deal with a difficult officer is to control yourself, and you will have a better chance of controlling the officer and the situation.

There are things a person can do to control situations in their life, like the following.

> Eliminate emotion; do not panic or run; remain calm; emotions may cause overreaction. Accept the situation for what it is; trying to prove another person wrong takes time and usually does not work. Do not take the situation to the extreme, turning a traffic stop into a felony.

When encountering law enforcement, do what the officer asks. Your life may depend on it! Too many videos taken by the public show a crime does not have to be committed for someone to die. These videos show how dangerous it is if an officer believes you are a threat or disrespects them.

The first requirement is understanding the situation; knowing the law can help. However, knowing the law differs from knowing what an officer can do. Most people have no clue about being in danger with law enforcement.

For instance, people insist an officer must read them their Miranda Warning. Police do not have to read your rights unless they want to use your words in court. Before taking you into custody, the officer must only say, "You are under arrest!" After the officer informs you of the arrest, uncooperative behavior is considered resisting. Officers defend wrongful actions by saying, "They did not follow my instruction and were resistive." Most arresting officers state, "You are being arrested," and place you in handcuffs and then in the back seat of their patrol vehicle without asking you any questions.

UNDERSTANDING THE OFFICER

The average person's opinion about the police comes from television, believing they know what officers go through or what they are thinking. Some believe the police never break the law, while others believe they are all heroes. Other citizens believe the greatest threat to them and their community is the police.

There are common beliefs, myths, and stereotypes about the police, like there is a "cop culture," one of corruption when it comes to taking care of each other, and the "thin blue line" or the "brotherhood." People believe the police like using force, or they would not have chosen policing as a career. They often believe officers have "cop" meetings to tell their war stories at some cop bar.

Officers usually do not interact with each other after work; officers are like any other employees. They rarely discuss what they do, especially with people, not friends or family. But hearing their war stories makes us feel the officers do not take their jobs with the proper care for those they meet.

Regardless of beliefs, the system may be unfair to citizens if the officer's department does not have an objective review board. Failure to be objective about police behavior or to correct their misconduct leads to the community scrutinizing the department.

The public scrutinizes police more than any other profession except politicians. This scrutiny weighs heavily on all officers but does not supersede the beliefs governing policing. Officers understand the high ethical standard they are held to and attempt to uphold this public trust.

Most officers operate professionally, even when faced with insults and those who dislike them for doing their jobs. When an officer gives a ticket, and the person admits to doing something wrong, it goes a long way in making the officer's day. Most officers have no desire to be confrontational; just like any employee, they want to do a good job. Officers view their jobs as routine and rarely get involved in a confrontation, leading to the use of deadly force. Few officers have never discharged their weapons during an encounter with the public. But when an officer is involved in a deadly encounter, their department attempts to help them overcome the traumatic feelings and emotions that occur with the incident.

What officers fear the most when involved in an officer shooting or misconduct is how long they are assigned to desk duty or placed on paid leave. Officers do not fear going to jail or losing their jobs. Officers lose their jobs for using drugs and domestic violence, not for misconduct while interacting with the public or for using excessive force.

The 1989 case of Graham v Conner influences how officers respond after an officer-involved shooting. (It influences excessive force.) This case allows an officer to shoot if they feel a potential threat to the officer's life. This response is called "the reasonably scared cop rule." If the officers can convince others they feel in danger and fearful, they have nothing to fear. Their actions do not have to reflect that the officer did anything to mitigate the situation; they only must feel fearful.

From 2005 till 2015, only fifty-four officers were prosecuted for shooting any citizen out of 10,000 shootings. Officers charged or investigated are usually acquitted because their defense is about lacking training and supervision, which helps maintain a distrust of law enforcement by too many communities.

The officer's defense is enhanced by how they are deployed and assigned to their patrol area. In small departments, police behavior is often due to them working alone, causing them to feel unsafe. An officer may have negative expectations when encountering a portion of the population and may approach these encounters cautiously. So, any negative response by the person confirms the officer's negative beliefs.

When an officer stops a citizen, particularly a citizen of color, the officer could be fearful of that person. The officer's feelings are like the rest of society, who fear encounters with members of a minority group. Too often, officers operate under the assumption the people they encounter are up to no good and are a danger to someone. These feelings are enhanced at the beginning of their shift during their daily briefing, where they are informed of the dangers they may encounter and how to handle them.

The officers' sense of fear may cause them to act impulsively or overreact to the actions of the person they stop. Most actions by police are appropriate, but when the officer's action is not within policy, for the behavior to continue, the officer must have the support of their peers and their department. The reason that minority people are treated differently than whites is more about policing than racism. The shooting of unarmed people happens all over the United States in the same unbelievable ways. Many, if not most, police supervisors and chiefs in large cities are Black individuals, many being Black women who enact and enforce the policies and procedures their officers enforce.

Departments often fail to hire officers from the community they patrol, which has enhanced the sense of fear and distrust in that community and eliminated the practice of community policing. Not being a part of the community may eliminate compassion toward that community. Community policing involves officers working where they go to church, school, and the market where they live.

Hiring black or brown officers to patrol black and brown communities does not stop mistreatment or corruption. If patrol groups like metro units in large cities lack care for those they interact with, the problem remains regardless of the officer's race.

The officer usually does not know the individual they encounter. If you do not have personal contact with the community, it is easy to hold negative beliefs about the person or community. Do they use the word community or neighborhood? The officer working in a neighborhood works in a geographic area of people. In contrast, an officer working in a community works with a class and type of person, a middle-class Black community vs. a Black gang neighborhood.

Officers who work with people they know and like are tolerant of their behavior and even humble when dealing with them. It is hard to meet an overly humble police officer, so being humble helps you control the situation by controlling yourself. For example, while committing a felony with a weapon, the best way to control this situation is to put the gun down, put your hands on your head, and go to the ground on your knees; running will get you shot.

STATISTICS

If you are frequently stopped, understand the statistics about your encounters. Police encounters are not random events; there is always a reason, just or unjust. The following are the percentages of stops by race, gender, and type of stops per year. These statistics come from the Bureau of Justice Statistics (BJS) from 2011.

The number of citizens stopped per year is 12% of the population. (About 5 million people) About 1% of drivers pulled over in traffic stops had physical force used against them by police. Of these drivers, 55% believed the police behaved properly during the stop. Over half of the people stopped, knew they had done something wrong, and became apologetic. Drivers who believed the stop was legitimate were pulled over by an officer of the same race or ethnicity; this was (83%). Drivers pulled over by an officer of a different race or ethnic origin believed the stop to be legitimate were about (74%).

Even though white drivers make up a larger portion of the driving population, they were both ticketed and searched at a lower rate than Black and Hispanic drivers.

The number one reason for contact with the police is a traffic stop. In 2011, an estimated 42% of face-to-face contacts U.S. residents had with police occurred for this reason. About half of all traffic stops resulted in a traffic ticket. Police searched approximately 3% of all drivers during their traffic stops.

An estimated 26.4 million people aged sixteen or older indicated their recent contact with the police was a traffic stop. Drivers reported speeding was usually the reason for being pulled over.

Approximately 80% of drivers pulled over felt it was for a legitimate reason. About 68% of black drivers believed police had a valid reason for stopping them compared to 84% of white and 74% of Hispanic drivers. In 2011, about 3% of traffic stops led to a search of the driver, the vehicle, or both. Police were more likely to search male drivers (4%) than female drivers (2%). A lower percentage of white drivers were searched (2%) than black (6%) or Hispanic (7%).

The value of these statistics helps to understand what the officer may expect when stopping a citizen, not what citizens should expect. Statistics do not provide what the officer thought during the encounter. Or provide us with the officer's emotions. They only provide the stop type and the officer's stated reason for the stop.

REASONABLE SUSPICION

The lack of a reason for a stop can make a person defensive; the officer does not see any reason for defensive behavior. When observing this behavior, the officer may become aggressive. Remaining calm and non-defensive (absent emotion) helps officers remain or return to their usual professional selves. Any officer showing emotion can be dangerous, and they may overreact to the encounter. Let the officer do what they must to accomplish their job is important.

The reason police can stop a citizen is that the officer has a reasonable belief or suspicion of a law violation unless they need your help. They can request or order you to let them use your vehicle. They cannot request your assistance if it places you in danger.

Suspicion starts when an officer observes the behavior or is informed of a violation so they can intervene. Police encounters should be based solely on behavior and void of beliefs or emotions. When officers are mistaken about the law, the courts may still view their actions as OK.

The Fourteenth Amendment says.

"No state shall make or enforce any law which shall abridge the privileges or immunities of citizens of the United States. Nor shall any state deprive any person of life, liberty, or property, without due process of law; nor deny to any person within its jurisdiction the equal protection of the laws." This statute gives a false belief that officers cannot detain or confiscate your property without due process. However, they can! When the officer asks for permission but does not get it, they must arrest and confiscate it. At some point, the officer must give a reason for taking it, which must be proven to be just.

The courts believe police need flexibility to act based on their information. Flexibility gives the police the right to do anything, fearing the situation or the person they encounter. The courts agreed that officers face dangerous situations, and under this standard, a search or seizure is permissible even when their action includes a factual mistake. Officers might, for example, stop a motorist for traveling alone in a high-occupancy vehicle lane, only to discover that two children are asleep in the back seat upon approaching the car.

But what if the police officer's reasonable mistake is not one of fact but of law? In this case, an officer stopped a vehicle because one of its two brake lights was out, but a court later determined that a single working brake light was all the law required. The question is whether such a mistake of law can give rise to the reasonable suspicion necessary to uphold the seizure under the Fourth Amendment. The officer's mistake about the brake-light law was reasonable, and the stop was lawful under the Fourth Amendment.

An example of this is Heien vs. North Carolina. This case affects how the police interact with the public.

On April 29, 2009, Sergeant Matt Darisse of the Surry County Sheriff's Department sat in his patrol car near Dobson, North Carolina, observing northbound traffic on Interstate 77. Shortly before 8 a.m., a Ford Escort passed by. Darisse said the driver looked "very stiff and nervous," so he pulled onto the interstate and began following the Escort. This officer did not pull the car over because the driver appeared nervous and could not view those emotions from where he was. A few miles down the road, the Escort braked as it approached a slower vehicle, but only the left brake light came on. Noting the faulty right brake light, Darisse activated his vehicle's lights and pulled the Escort over. Two men were in the car: Maynor Javier Vasquez sat behind the wheel, and petitioner

Nicholas Brady Heien lay across the rear seat. Sergeant Darisse explained to Vasquez that if his license and registration checked out, he would receive only a warning ticket for the broken brake light. A records check revealed no problems with the documents, and Darisse gave Vasquez the warning ticket.

But Darisse had become suspicious during the stop—Vasquez appeared nervous, Heien remained lying down the entire time, and the two gave inconsistent answers about their destination. Darisse asked Vasquez if he would answer some questions. Vasquez assented, and Darisse asked whether the men were transporting various types of contraband. He said no. Darisse asked whether he could search for the Escort. Vasquez said he had no objection but told Darisse he should ask Heien because Heien owned the car. Heien gave his consent, and Darisse, aided by a fellow officer who had since arrived, began a thorough search of the vehicle. In the side compartment of a duffle bag, Darisse found a bag containing cocaine. The officers arrested both men.

The fact the officer asked for permission indicated that he wanted to do what he could to search for this vehicle. Fear is an acceptable emotion, usually held by the officer, and should not be held by a citizen. A police stop is not usually a violation of rights, but what the officer does after the stop may become a violation. Most officers experience a small amount of fear based on a reasonable safety concern. The officer operates based on reasonable belief or suspicion of the person they are encountering. This concept of reasonable belief and suspicion must fit the situation,

Officers who know that a crime is in progress may use their power to give an order. They may ask for assistance, but saying no is okay; however, they will expect your cooperation. In some situations, refusing to assist is an obstruction and an arrest can be made for not providing it. In ordering cooperation, the officer gains evidence in several ways.

One way to get evidence is to use informants. The principle for enforcing cooperation agreements with informants arises under the due process clause of the Fourteenth Amendment. This fundamental fairness requires respecting promises made during plea bargaining and similar contexts.

Cooperation agreements are construed strictly against the government, and the confidential informant agreement should not be in writing. Whether the agreement is in writing or conveyed verbally, police officers can bind the prosecution to an enforceable resolution by their words.

To prevent the agreement from being denied later, it should be in writing to eliminate ambiguous meanings, especially when those words are relied upon to persuade a defendant to act in exchange for the dismissal of pending charges. Defendants must make full confessions to their crimes. In exchange, the state agrees that confidential informant charges are dropped or dismissed. It is a due process violation to allow the police or the prosecution to exploit a confidential informant, have that person incriminate themselves, and then charge the informant with their crimes. If this is done, the defendant may file a motion to dismiss to enforce their agreement with the police.

With the information the informant has provided the officer on their new investigation, they may act; they now have more than reasonable suspicion the other suspect has committed, is committing, or is about to commit a crime.

Many things can influence the officer to gain evidence other than having someone provide information, such as the officer feeling in danger and knowing that a crime is about to be committed.

Officers do not work under a cloud of fear all day, but getting an officer to stop being fearful is not easy. Knowing what the officers view as a threat helps to deal with the situation. The lack of fear is attributed to a feeling of comfort. To understand the lack of fear, look at situations where officers are not usually fearful. Often, when an officer stops a white female, the older the female is, the safer the situation. It is not common to see a white woman with her hands in the air or arresting her face down on the ground. For this to happen, a weapon is seen or used and is still in the woman's possession. The profile of this person does not pose a threat to the officer.

It is human nature to view what is different with suspicion. A citizen detained should appear normal and non-threatening to gain the desired response from the officer. No one should be viewed as a threat in non-threatening situations.

Would it be reasonable for an officer to stop and question a q while jogging? The officer's actions and questions reflect their beliefs. Where were you running? What were you carrying? A reasonable person interprets you as jogging, not running, based on your clothing. In this situation, address the reason for the stop. Why is there a problem? Inform the officer their actions were unreasonable, and you will file a complaint.

 "Reasonable Suspicion" factual circumstances that lead a reasonable police officer or person to believe criminal activity may occur." All officers' actions to stop and detain should be based on this rule.

When the officers' actions are unreasonable, they may state, "Based on my experience, I needed to do what I did," to make their actions meet the legal form of suspicion. Many courts allow the officer to act based on facts or circumstances caused by an officer's training and experience. Reasonable suspicion is more than a guess or hunch but less than Probable Cause.

For an officer to meet the probable cause standard test, the evidence must be present, i.e., a statement to the officer, contraband in view, or possible physical evidence. If the stop-and-frisk gives probable cause to believe the detainee has committed a crime, then the officer can make an arrest.

"Suspicion" is a question or belief, and "Cause" is the source or foundation of any belief. There should always be cause for suspicion. A person walking down the street at noon with no crime in progress does not provide a cause for suspicion. So, anytime an officer makes a stop or confiscates property and fails to give the cause of the officer's action, the evidence may be excluded.

The rationale behind the Supreme Court's decisions on the probable cause of exclusionary rule revolves around the understanding, as the opinion notes, "The exclusionary rule has its limitations." This rule states without probable cause, the evidence collected cannot be presented in court. The rule aims to protect persons from unreasonable searches and seizures aimed at gathering evidence, not searches and seizures for other purposes (like crime prevention or personal protection of police officers). The amendments and rulings direct the police stops, and the profiling process does not meet these standards.

The only way to correct an officer's mistreatment is to destroy the officer's reasonable suspicion statement. One way of doing this is to show that the officer was biased and had no reason to act.

Profiling

The concept of profiling involves information based on a biased interpretation of facts. Everyone enters a situation with their opinions, beliefs, and expectations influencing their actions. Officers' expectations should be based solely on their experience and training in identifying criminal behavior.

For law enforcement, there are two major types of profiling. Racial Profiling and Offender Profiling

Racial profiling targets a person of a particular race based on a stereotype about their race. Racial profiling occurs when a police officer stops, questions, arrests, and searches someone solely based on the person's race or ethnicity. Racial profiling usually involves stopping ethnic groups based on the probability of being involved in criminal behavior.

> African Americans – are involved in gangs, assault, and drugs,
> Asian Americans – are involved in espionage,
> Hispanics and Latinos – are involved in illegal immigration and drug gangs,
> Arabs and Muslims/South are involved in Terrorism, and
> Jews – are involved in conspiracy and white-collar crimes.

Offender or criminal profiling is a tool law enforcement uses to identify suspects (descriptive offender profiling) and analyze patterns that may predict future offenses and victims (predictive offender profiling). In many cases, offender profiling starts with or considers race and ethnic background. Race is only part of an offender profile when members of that race are the only ones perpetrating the crime. Hate crimes are usually a race crime, where the actions are targeted towards a particular race by another race.

For profiling to be offender profiling, the following five steps are included.

> Analyzing the criminal act and comparing it to similar crimes in the past,
> An in-depth analysis of the actual crime scene,
> Considering the background and activities for motives and connections,
> Considering other motives and
> Developing a description of the offender can be compared with previous cases.

Officers state they only engage in offender profiling, viewed as effective policing. Whenever an officer stops someone, some form of profiling occurs based on suspicion. The officers believe they have "just cause" to act in these situations. Right or wrong, we are at the mercy of the police, and officers can justify anything they do. It is better to go to court than to the hospital or worse.

ENCOUNTERS

Both sides of any encounter approach the situation based on past beliefs about what will happen. The contract of common beliefs should cause both parties to behave expectedly. The officer must be professional, and the citizen must be orderly and respectful. Police encounters fall under three situations.

> Unexpected,
> Routine,
> Crime in progress.

Controlling encounters is based on expectations.

> When you encounter an unexpected situation, being at the market, having coffee at Starbucks, or gassing up your vehicle, always start by explaining the surprise you are dealing with.
>
> The most common officer encounter is a routine traffic stop; both sides feel they know what may happen.
>
> Based on emotions on both sides, the responses may be inciting. Follow all instructions.

Some beliefs may cause a particular response.

> If the officer feels the citizen has a weapon, they are likely to be told to go to the ground. If the officer feels threatened,
> they are likely to use force.

When stopped, there are things to keep in mind, like a "To-Do List;"

> The police officer is in charge.
> Police officers often think individuals they encounter are potential threats.
> Do not act in a threatening manner or make sudden movements.
> Treat the officer with respect, kindness, and courtesy, and do not insult or talk back.
> Officers respond negatively to rudeness, arrogance, or insults.
> Know your rights as a citizen.
> If the encounter is problematic, tell the officer you are recording it before asking questions.
> If there are witnesses, get their names and contact information, and try to get witnesses of diverse ethnic groups if possible.
> When asked to get out of the car, do not ask why; take your keys, place them in your pocket, or hold them and lock them as you exit.

Dangerous confrontations may lead to violence and can be avoided with common sense.

There are things never to do.

> Do not yell,
> Do not run or walk toward an officer without being told to do so,
> Do not run away,

If your hands are in your pockets, do not remove them until told to do so,
Do not make any threatening gestures,
Do not joke,
Try not to be disrespectful.

Doing the following, you go to jail.

Driving drunk or drug possession
Being the aggressor in a domestic call
Actively committing a felony

Regular encounters with law enforcement and having an attorney on retainer are mandatory. It is important to know who to call as soon as possible, so call your lawyer.

People make the mistake of reacting negatively or in an aggressive manner when confronted by police. Usually, the person feels they are treated unfairly. Unfortunately, such a reaction can lead to arrests, rough handling by the police, or even being fatally shot.

When an officer encounters a negative attitude or dislikes a person, he or she is more likely to overreact to the situation. If the officer has a problem, the officer may authoritatively approach with a defensive stance, standing off to the side and not directly in front. Their tone is aggressive.

When this occurs, ask the officer, "Sir, what did I do?' or "Sir, I may be wrong, but why are you upset?" Regardless of the answer, do what they ask. The officer may not be offended by the question and may realize they are overreacting to something.

It is not wise to think of the officer as a racist or to believe they do not respect you. They may not understand their actions and how others view them. The officer may be fearful for reasons you may not understand. They may have information about a crime or situation, believing you are a person of interest.

Do not insult the officer by asking, "What is your problem?" Ask, "What is wrong? What do you need me to do? Once the reason for the stop or encounter is given, attempt to control it. Admitting to a traffic violation with a reason for the offense may allow the officer to change the violation or not give a ticket.

SEARCHES

From early childhood, we believe no one should go through or search our stuff without our permission, believing we have a right to privacy, as stated in the constitution.

But we will allow the police to search us and our property, feeling we do not have a choice. We do not want the police to feel we are doing something wrong. So, we say things like, "Yes, go ahead; I have nothing to hide."

Officers may be on shaky ground when they ask for permission to do something instead of requiring as teenagers; we hated letting our parents search our room, knowing we had nothing to hide. Remember, people do not ask if they do not need to do it! So, never permit a police officer to search your car or home without a warrant.

To get permission, the officer often says you match the description of some suspect and need to search to eliminate you as a suspect. Saying no, they must arrest you to continue. They must now tell the truth, or the evidence is not allowed.

Once the search has started, it is hard to stop it, regardless of how it is conducted. If the search is necessary, the officer does what it takes to search legally.

We have a right to privacy. However, the expectation of privacy in a car is less than in your home. Because of this lessened expectation, the police can conduct a warrantless vehicle search if the officer has probable cause. The police officer may lie about what they call probable cause. Believing this to be the case, whatever is found would not be admissible in court.

Remember the officer's reason for the search; if the reason was that the officer could see an item, make sure they could. Take a picture of your car from where the officer could look.

If an officer attempts to use force to search, do not resist; back away and inform them of your objections to the search, and due to the use of force, the search may not be legal.

The officer should not request to search your car for a traffic violation. No routine traffic violations are a reason for a vehicle search. However, if the officer saw you throw an empty beer bottle (or any item) out the window, this is sufficient probable cause to search your vehicle.

If the officer "thinks" they smell marijuana as they approach the car, they may use probable cause to search your vehicle. There is not much you can do. If the "I smell" reason is given, taking a blood test or urine test to prove you were not under the influence of any drug may help your case, but this may not prove the officer did not smell what they said they smelled.

Consent Searches

Officers need your permission to search without a warrant. Police often go to the owner or manager for access to a residence and permission to search. When the person in charge of the premises freely and voluntarily agrees to the search, the officer must limit the search to evidence related to their suspicion. If the police limit their search to whatever the person agreed to, the search will usually be valid.

Courts do not always require the police to ask for permission before searching each room or object; they often find the initial consent was broad enough to justify whatever search the officers conducted, so long as the police officer's interpretation of the consent was reasonable. For example, if a tenant consents to search their "house," a court may determine that a reasonable interpretation of "house" includes rooms, closets, attics, and basements within the dwelling.

A reasonable interpretation of "house" may not include vehicles, backyard storage sheds, detached greenhouses, or any buildings or property outside the dwelling. Courts would consider consent valid if the police believed the consenting person had the authority to consent, even if it turned out they did not. Courts often rule that one's consent is enough to search at least some parts of the premises if there are two or more tenants in one dwelling.

Search Made in Connection with an Arrest

A police officer does not need a warrant to search "incident to" an arrest. After a lawful arrest, an officer can search the arrestee and the area within the arrestee's immediate control, like your car.

Police may make what is known as a "protective sweep" or "called an area search" of the premises following an arrest. They can "sweep" if they suspect a dangerous co-conspirator might be hiding in the area. The officer typically looks in spaces immediately next to the area of the arrest that may hold a hidden attacker.

A protective sweep should be limited to a cursory visual inspection of places where an accomplice might hide. For example, police officers can often look under beds and inside closets. If a sweep is lawful, the police can seize contraband or evidence of a crime in plain sight during the sweep. However, the sweep must protect the officers, not gather evidence.

The Emergency Exception

As a rule, the police are authorized to conduct a warrantless search when the time it would take to get a warrant would jeopardize public safety or lead to the loss of relevant evidence. Here are some situations in which most judges would uphold a warrantless search:

Following a street drug arrest, an officer enters the house after the suspect shouts, "John, quick, flush it!" The officer arrests John and seizes the stash.

The officer on routine patrol hears shouts and screams coming from a residence, rushes in, and arrests a suspect for spousal abuse. They can arrest if in "hot pursuit" of a fleeing felon and continue the chase into the suspect's dwelling. An officer's duty to protect people and preserve evidence outweighs the warrant requirement in these emergencies.

The Fourth Amendment can go against you. The Amendment does permit searches, and seizures are reasonable. In practice, the police may override your privacy concerns and search your home, barn, car, boat, office, personal or business documents, bank account records, trash barrel, or whatever.

The police have probable cause to believe they can find evidence a crime was committed, and a judge issues a warrant or circumstances justify the search without a warrant first being issued.

When the Fourth Amendment Does Not Protect You

The Fourth Amendment applies to searching only if a person has a "legitimate expectation of privacy" in the place or thing searched. If not, the amendment offers no protection; there are no privacy issues. Courts use a two-part test (fashioned by the U.S. Supreme Court) to determine whether, at the time of the search, a defendant had a legitimate expectation of privacy in the place or things searched:

Did the person expect some degree of privacy?
Is the person's expectation objectively reasonable—one that society recognizes?

For example, an individual who uses a public restroom expects not to be spied upon (the person expects privacy). Most people, including judges, consider this expectation objectively reasonable. Installing a hidden video camera by the police in a public restroom would be considered an "illegal search" and the Fourth Amendment's reasonableness requirement.

The Supreme Court has continually asserted the rule officers must be given the "benefit of the doubt" if they acted lawfully in carrying out their day-to-day duties, a position reasserted in Saucier v. Katz.

An excellent example of how these works comes from a Supreme Court case in which the court held that a bus passenger had a legitimate expectation of privacy in an opaque carry-on bag positioned in a luggage rack above the passenger's head. The Court held that physical probing by the police of the bag's exterior for evidence of contraband constituted a search subject to Fourth Amendment limitations.

Once your property is secured, it is assumed that you have a right to privacy. On the other hand, if an officer stops a car and notices a weapon on the passenger seat when talking to the driver, there has been no search under the Fourth Amendment. If the driver somehow considers the passenger seat a private place, society is unwilling to extend the protections to this location. In other words, there is no objectively reasonable expectation of privacy regarding the gun in plain view.

Get Help

If you are arrested or charged with a crime or want to know how the law applies to your situation, consult an experienced criminal defense lawyer. The law can vary from state to state, and a knowledgeable lawyer can adequately explain it. If you want or need a criminal defense lawyer, go to Nolo's trusted Lawyer Directory to find one near you.

Body Searches Pat Downs/Frisk

Under the stop-and-frisk exception, the police can stop and pat anyone down for anything illegal if they have a suspicion.

When properly detained, the police will ask for ID; you may be arrested in some states for refusing to give it. If you fear giving your ID is incriminating, claim the right to remain silent; this may be a defense if arrested. Refusing to answer questions is not a crime but might make the police suspicious.

The police may think they have a reason (probable cause) to stop and ask questions. Being detained or arrested may depend on how calm and prepared you are. Make sure your actions are non-threatening.

There is a difference between a stop leading to a frisk and one leading to a search. The law governing these procedures is Terry v. Ohio. This stop and frisk may be called a Terry Stop.

Terry v. Ohio, 392 U.S. was a landmark decision by the United States Supreme Court. The court stated that, under Terry, the Fourth Amendment prohibition on unreasonable searches and seizures is not violated when a police officer stops a suspect on the street and frisks him or her without probable cause to arrest him or her but for mere suspicion and the officer's safety.

This case came about because the New York Police Department initiated a policy where their officers could stop anyone, and they wanted to stop because suspicion was not needed. In this procedure, the officer could stop someone they wanted to check for a weapon.

One problem with Terry and its application is no crime needs to be in progress. The officer only needs to say, "You look suspicious and may have a weapon." Suspicion is entirely up to the officer's interpretation. In 2013, the procedure was ruled unconstitutional; it was deemed racial profiling because most of those frisked were minority citizens.

Terry has not gone away; many police departments now use a procedure to search based only on suspicion to find cash.

In many airports and other locations in America, local police, not TSA, are stopping people at their gates to search for Drugs. The reality is they are searching to find large amounts of cash.

It is difficult to track cash transactions, so the US government, over the last 35 years, has quietly enacted civil forfeiture laws that make it possible for police to confiscate cash or other property with near-zero evidence of any wrongdoing. The states that do not have their confiscation law will use federal civil forfeiture laws to confiscate cash or other property and receive a kickback of up to 80% from the federal government.

When the government seizes your property under a civil forfeiture law, it does not need to prove guilt. All it needs is evidence that your property is subject to forfeiture.

US courts have repeatedly ruled that possession of a large sum of cash is "strong evidence" of a connection to trafficking drugs. The courts feel possessing a large sum of cash is sufficient evidence to seize it unless evidence is that it is not connected to illegal activity. The practice can be done with any stops made by law enforcement.

Possessing a large amount of cash, usually exceeding $10,000, but in some cities, it may be less than $100, you may lose it as the probable proceeds of a narcotics transaction. They do not need to make an arrest or present any evidence of narcotics involvement to keep your money.

Stopping young males or people who dress in a manner that appears to represent being a drug user or dealer and asking to search them is increasing all over the United States. Since 911, in airports, we feel we have no choice when interacting with law enforcement who ask us for ID or to submit to a search. It has become more important that you say "No."

Being in an airport means you are on a schedule, and the officers know this. If the officer does not have probable cause to stop and search, they may allow you to continue because of the number of witnesses.

Hopefully, there will be witnesses when a request to search is made, and the officer uses force. Because after **using force, some officers may claim, "You went for a weapon."**

Think carefully about your words, movements, body language, and emotions. Do not get into an argument. Remember, even if a Miranda Warning is not given and an arrest is not made, anything said or done can be used. What you say can be interpreted in a way you did not mean. Your words and actions may be the reason for the further actions.

It is frustrating for officers to deal with people who refuse to say anything at all to any question. But be prepared to go to jail; your behavior will make the officer even more suspicious. Deciding not to talk to the officer should only be done after saying no or arresting me.

Any frisk should only be used to detect concealed weapons, not for contraband. When an officer frisks someone and fails to detect a weapon, the officer cannot go into your pocket or have you remove items that are not weapons.

If other evidence, such as a suspected drug container, can be felt under the suspect's clothing, it can be seized by the officer later. This procedure is called the "plain feel" doctrine or "plain view." To pass the plain feel test, the item must have an immediately apparent character or quality of being contraband or evidence. To retrieve the item, an arrest must be made. A frisk is justified under the following circumstances:

Concern for the safety of the officer or others.

Suspicion: the suspect is armed and dangerous.

Suspicion: the suspect is about to commit a crime where a weapon is commonly used.

The officer is alone, and their backup has not arrived.

The number of suspects present and their physical size, Behavior, emotional state, and looking for suspects; the suspect gave evasive answers during the initial stop, time of day, and geographical surroundings (not sufficient by themselves to justify frisk).

The officer wants to talk and frisk you; they must have a reasonable belief in the presence of a weapon. However, you should ask, am I being arrested? Do not allow the search if the officer says no. Ask to leave.

If they make an arrest, they will handcuff and search. If they fail to find contraband, they must allow you to leave without jailing you. Any arrest may violate your rights, such as a false arrest. You will need to prove the arrest was only to search.

Allowing the frisk, maintain your right to silence. Usually, you will be asked, "Where are you headed?" Respond to this question: "If I am not being arrested, I am free to leave?"

Sometimes, police say, "No, you are not being arrested. We have questions." Saying yes, they are free to ask to pat you down for their safety. Again, say "No."

Asking to leave instead of being questioned eliminates the officer's safety threat. Since they are suspects in a new crime, they will start over but still do not give permission for any search or answer questions.

However, the officer may only pat your outer clothing for weapons if the search is allowed. This search is for their safety.

If the officer finds a weapon, they will handcuff you and go into your pockets. Otherwise, a police officer cannot make you empty your pockets or go through your pockets unless they make an arrest.

To protect yourself, make it clear you "do not consent to a search" and ask for the reason; remember the reason given.

During a frisk, do not move or talk to the officer!

Not knowing your rights to refuse a search may be a factor in determining whether your consent was voluntary. If an officer inappropriately touches you, make a written complaint.

Often, citizens believe the police must inform them of their intentions. The Court has reasoned that the police do not need to give warnings, as warnings might detract from the informality of a routine interaction between civilians and the police.

OBSERVATIONS

States require an objective or unbiased observation by the officer to search or detain. The search is not a judgment call by the officer about your actions. Their observation must be based on objective standards of evidence to be reasonable. In a court proceeding, the judge's feeling about the search may be based on an argument about whose version of the facts is correct.

For instance, if cited for failing to stop at a red light or for making a prohibited turn, who wins the case will depend on whom the judge believes. The guy wearing the badge usually wins unless you can cast doubt on their ability to perceive accurately what happened. Some techniques may raise at least a reasonable doubt about guilt. Having other unbiased witnesses may go a long way to help your cause.

Here are the types of evidence most likely to convince the judge you were right:

Statements from witnesses, such as passengers or bystanders, who testify to your version of events.

A clear, easy-to-understand diagram showing where you and the officer's vehicle were to key locations and objects, such as an intersection, traffic signal, or another vehicle. Diagrams are important for tickets given at intersections, such as right-of-way, traffic lights, or stop sign violations.

Photographs of intersections, stop signs, and road conditions can show conditions like obscured stop signs or other physical evidence to support your case.

Other evidence would cause doubt about the officer's ability to accurately observe your alleged violation. A classic way to do this is to prove the officer's position made it impossible to see what happened.

One of the greatest pieces of evidence is the officers' dash-cam when activated. There are three ways for an officer to activate the camera: automatically flipping on the overhead lights, manually turning the camera on inside the car, or activating a wireless microphone outside the car. In some states, officers must notify citizens that a voice recording is made. The officer's actions should be questioned in court if the cameras were not activated.

Mistake of Fact

Judges may give leeway in considering circumstances beyond your control. Showing you made an honest and reasonable error, a judge might find you made a "mistake of fact," meaning your ticket should be dismissed. Provide evidence to prove your point; take pictures or provide witnesses.

Here are several examples:

> Failing to stop before coming to the pedestrian crosswalk markers because they were old, faded, and could not be seen. Take a picture at the time of the day of the citation.

> Failure to stop at a stop sign after a major storm because a broken branch hid the sign. Please take pictures of the obscured sign and show them to the judge to support your argument.

This argument often comes down to claiming that fair notice was not given for the expected conduct. For example, a judge might dismiss a ticket for running a stop sign if it was brand new. However, the judge would not buy this defense if:

> Has the sign been up for more than a few weeks?
> You had never stopped at the intersection (and, therefore, should not be fooled by its sudden presence), or You were speeding.

A mistake of fact can be caused by believing your actions were justified, considering the circumstances of your alleged violation. For example, being charged with driving too slowly (ten miles under the speed limit) in the left lane is a legal defense in all states if you had to slow down to make a legal left turn.

A successful defense raises additional facts or a legal point rather than simply contradicting the officer's testimony.

Examples:

> If forced to stop on a freeway because your car has become unsafe to continue driving, give a repair bill, or you had a physical or medical problem and needed to get to a doctor.

Emergencies not of your making may be another legal "necessity" defense recognized in all fifty states. To make an extreme example, beating a speeding charge proves you increased speed to avoid a truck. The key here is to convincingly argue you were forced to violate the exact wording of traffic law to avoid a severe and immediate danger to yourself or others.

Here are some examples:

> You were driving in the right or slow lane and were boxed in from the back and left side by other cars. You accelerated to avoid colliding with a car entering the highway from the right.

> A car is to the right, and you briefly speed up to avoid being rear-ended by a super-aggressive big rig that was tailgating. Once in the clear, you move to the right and resume at a legal speed.

Your reason for swerving across a double yellow line is to avoid hitting another vehicle, pedestrian, animal, or unexpected obstacle. If you had failed to take evasive action, you would have been at high risk of being involved in an accident. (This may not be the case if you were speeding)

However, it is important to realize the difference between presenting a necessity defense based on road conditions and producing an excuse for breaking the law based on inattention or personal need.

WHEN DETAINED

If someone knocks on your door, even when you believe it is the police, ask who it is. Before opening the door, always put your foot about three inches at the bottom edge as a wedge to prevent the person from pushing through. This procedure will help prevent a home invasion.

If the police ask to enter your home, do not open the door without a warrant. If the officer has no warrant and you are alone, step outside to talk and close the door; do not lock it. If you are looking out to see the police and you do not answer the officer, they may call for backup and make a forced entry.

You do not have to go with the police unless they arrest you. Say so if you do not want to answer their questions or go with them. If you believe the officer has "just cause" for the interaction, cooperate and follow orders. However, do not answer questions or converse with the officer or others until you have discussed the matter with a lawyer.

Never play lawyer; tell the officer you have nothing to say and leave it at that. Do not lecture the police on the law; all officers know your constitutional rights.

If the police have a search warrant, ask to see it and have them pass the warrant through the door. Read it closely and remember it is yours to keep. Ensure it is signed with the correct date, address, and apartment number. The warrant should state the items to be retrieved. Once receiving the warrant, allow them to come in to do their job. Often, the officer searches to locate witnesses and to get evidence, and they hope to get further information about an incident.

If you have questions about the officer's identity, ask to see their ID. Do not take the uniform as proof; view their ID card.

Be suspicious of individuals not in uniform or an official car. A flashing light on a vehicle does not make it a police car.

If you become suspicious, call their station to verify their position and the reason for detaining you. A legitimate or "real" officer has no problem with this, while an imposter will say no.

In some emergencies (when a person screams for help, the police chase a suspect, or they receive a 911 call), officers can enter and search your home without a warrant. Your cooperation is mandatory in these situations. Still, ask questions at home, but do not interfere with the officer.

In an unexpected encounter with the police, assume the officer suspects you of a crime. Listen to the officers' questions and get as much information as possible. Then, respond to questions unless they seem unreasonable or unusual. I, you are the subject, asked for the reason for the investigation.

The Fifth Amendment states.

"No person shall be held to answer for a capital, or otherwise infamous crime, unless on a presentment or indictment of a grand jury, except in cases arising in the land or naval forces, or in the militia, when in actual service in time of war or public danger; nor shall any person be subject for the same offense to be twice put in jeopardy of life or limb; nor shall be compelled in any criminal case to be a witness against himself, nor be deprived of life, liberty, or property, without due process of law; nor shall private property be taken for public use, without just compensation."

Stops

We must look at stops in greater detail. A stop is a seizure of a person. There are two types of stops:

A show of force stop is done with an officer physically putting their hands on the person with the intent of detaining or arresting them.

A show-of-authority stop occurs when the officer's request, demeanor, and display of authority persuade a person to submit to the stop. The key element in this type of stop is that the individual must submit to the show of authority, believing they are compelled to cooperate. When the officer identifies themselves and shows their ID, it is an authority stop.

A stop is justified if the suspect exhibits any combination of the following behaviors:

It appears not to fit the time or place.
Matches the description on a "Wanted" flyer.
Acts strangely or is emotional, angry, fearful, or intoxicated.
Loitering and looking as if they may commit a crime.
Running away or engaging in furtive movements.
Present in a crime scene area.
Present in a high-crime area and loitering.

When stopped for these reasons, the officer should inform you that you are being arrested; otherwise, they would not have made the stop. Often, the stop may seem wrong or unfair, but the officer believes they have a reason.

Concealed Weapon Permit

"Concealed weapon" refers to handguns, kept hidden from one's person and under control. Carrying a concealed weapon is illegal in most states unless the party with the weapon is a law enforcement officer or has a concealed weapon permit. Citizens receive training and must pass a class to carry concealed.

When an off-duty officer or a person with a concealed weapon permit is stopped, the detained officer or person should do certain things.

One is to identify as an officer or a person with a carry permit.

Two inform the detaining officer they are armed and where the weapon is.

It must be done in this order, or the detaining officer may draw their weapon when someone says, "I am armed."

Having a weapon with a legal right to carry, and you are stopped, keep your hands in the officer's view and tell the officer, "I have a permit to carry," wait for the officer to respond before saying, "I am armed." This response may eliminate the officer from having you go to

the ground or draw their weapon. This behavior shows the officer you have their safety in mind.

Police officers consider and understand two things when dealing with the public.

The attitude of the suspect,

Expectations of the stop.

The outcome is usually safe when these stops go as the officer expects.

Showing ID

No law requires you to carry a government I.D. unless you drive a car. In 24 states, police may require you to identify yourself, and if you are suspected of a crime, you can be arrested for not identifying yourself, like having a credit card or student ID. Once an officer has your I.D., you do not have to answer any more questions.

As soon as an officer asks you a question and you feel there may be a problem with this officer, ask the officer, "Are you arresting me, and Am I Free to go?" Request to see a lawyer if you are detained or arrested.

Never argue or insult an officer, stay calm, and watch your body language and emotions. Keep your hands where the officer can see them.

If the officer is abusive, ask for their "supervisor" at your location. If the officer refuses to call, say no more. There is no telling what this officer may do!

Traffic Stops

The largest number of police interactions occur while a person is in their vehicle. To operate a vehicle, you need the standard documentation of a driver's license, registration, and proof of insurance. If your license is expired or revoked and you are driving a vehicle, you risk losing your right to operate a vehicle or being arrested if you are involved in an accident.

Any questions other than requesting your documentation is for the officer's safety. When a traffic officer stops you for a violation, your attitude is your best defense. Turn your car off and turn on your vehicle's interior lights at night. Remove your sunglasses or hat and place your hands on the steering wheel at 10 and 2 (o'clock).

You may be advised to put your keys on the roof of your car as a sign of total submission. (If you do this, you cannot prevent them from taking your keys and entering your vehicle without your permission)

Always be respectful and non-threatening. Opening your window more than a crack to hand the officer any requested items is not mandatory. By doing this, some officers may feel you are hiding something. If the officer asks you to lower the window more, ask why they stopped you, and do not resist. Do not move or search around in your car, which might make the officer suspicious.

Get permission to move around in your vehicle. Never, ever get out of the car until instructed to do so! The point of these actions is to take any unnecessary tension out of the encounter. Imagine the types of people and the dangers officers face; do not be a negative part of their lives.

Wait for the officer to ask questions. A standard question they may ask "Do you know why I stopped you?" and your answer should be polite. The second question is, "Do you know you did??????" How you answer may determine what happens next. Do you get a warning or a ticket? If you were speeding and you know it, some officers love honesty, and this may make a difference. "Yes, I did, but I did not realize I was going fast because I was. ----"

Many stops are due to a problem with your vehicle, like in the Heien case. Stopping you does not allow the Officers to search your vehicle. However, the officer stated that their stop was reasonable and legal. Observing the officers' actions says a lot about the stop. The street or patrol officers in uniform may not identify themselves.

As the officer approaches, look in your rearview mirror; this will tell you about the stop. Does the officer unhook their weapon? Does the officer stand where you cannot see them? The officer's actions let you know they feel threatened and are testing your responses to the questions that will follow.

During traffic stops, if the officer has not stated the reason for the stop, the officer may ask questions such as, where are you going? Where have you been and to see who, and how long was the visit? The officer is fishing to find something against you! Their questions may attempt to see if you have been drinking and how much, as well as how nervous you get, which may indicate something more serious.

No law requires citizens to provide information about their legal activities! If the stop was because your vehicle matches one in a crime, they should say so.

If ordered out of your car, take your keys and lock the door behind you. Now, the officer should give their reason for entering your vehicle. You may say you object unless arrested. You may request they do not enter your vehicle. If they insist on giving you the keys, anything they retrieve is not admissible in court.

In certain cases, your car can be searched without a warrant if the police have probable cause, like being under the influence. To protect yourself, ensure you do not consent to a search. An arrest should not be made simply for refusing to give consent.

Planning to fight a ticket, answer "yes" or "no" to their questions. Do not give long, complicated answers. Have a good reason for any violation, like having a physical problem or emergency. Contesting the ticket, submit a letter claiming your innocence, and the police officer may do the same. If you lose, ask for an in-person trial, request traffic school, or pay penalties or fines.

When pleading "not guilty," you are assigned to a court to continue the trial. You can get your case dismissed if the officer does not show up. However, in cities with a large turnout, the judge can reduce your offense to lesser charges by reducing points on your driving records, or in county ordinances, no points will be placed on your record.

Once the ticket has been signed, the traffic stop is over. If you want to stand around, "shoot the breeze," and have fun, do it; you may see them again.

Once the officer gets your information, ask politely and talk to them about the violation.

If you break the law, admit it and tell the officer he was justified in pulling you over. Officers take pride in their work and love to know they are doing a good job, and sometimes, they do not feel it necessary to punish you any further. The better you make the officer feel, the more likely he will let you go; it is possible.

Stopped for speeding, asked to see the radar, and then asked questions about its use. Many jurisdictions require the officer to allow you to see the radar. Do not press it if the officer says no. You might ask, "When was the last time your radar gun was calibrated?" or "Where were you when you clocked my speed?" or "Were you moving when you clocked my speed?"

Do not ask these questions in an argumentative tone or sarcastically.

The DUI Stop

Driving Under the Influence (DUI) differs from getting stopped for speeding, where an officer gives you a ticket with a court date. Anyone drinking and driving risks harming others so that they may be arrested and taken to jail. The average driver who drank and drove and was unfortunate enough to get stopped usually got stopped at a checkpoint they could not avoid.

A person stopped on suspicion of drunk driving; the officer asked first, have you been drinking? If you know you are over the limit and cannot pass the upcoming test, remain silent, say "yes," or say, "I'd rather not say." Telling the officer, "Yes, I had two beers," to be prepared to take a test. It is always wise to have no more than two drinks about 45 minutes apart; two drinks in two hours are OK.

Being suspected of Driving Under the Influence, law enforcement has three primary ways to test for Blood Alcohol. (breathalyzer), a urine test, or a blood test.

Suppose an officer has obtained a warrant to have you submit to a **Blood Alcohol Content (BAC)** test. In all states, you must submit to the test.

The officer did not advise you of the consequences of a chemical test refusal. Your refusal resulted from an injury (that was not caused or contributed to by alcohol or drugs).

In some states, refusing to submit to a blood alcohol test has different consequences. In some states, you have a right to refuse a blood alcohol test with no additional penalties; in some, you will face penalties beyond your DUI charges.

Regardless of refusing the test at the scene, the police may still arrest you and request that you submit to a blood or urine test once you are at the station. Even in jurisdictions that allow refusal of the breathalyzer test, there are penalties for refusing to submit to a blood or urine test.

Should the officer believe you are over the limit, the test begins. The office starts the (DUI) process; the officer asks you to step out of the vehicle and perform a test referred to as the Standardized Field Sobriety Test (SFST).

Usually, there are two tests. The first is the "walk-and-turn." In this test, you must walk a line, one foot in front of the other, while taking nine steps in each direction. The officer administers the next test, the "stand on one leg." After the officer has determined whether they feel you were driving intoxicated, they may place you under arrest and take you to the station for the official BAC test.

Blood Alcohol Content (BAC) is 0.08%. The three most common tests for BAC are breath, blood, and urine. Many states require a breath test but allow you to request a blood or urine test. Knowing your state's requirements if you choose to drink and drive is important.

BAC Breath Test

Breath testing is a common method law enforcement uses to estimate blood levels. BAC breath analysis devices or breathalyzers are lightweight, portable, and provide immediate results.

BAC Blood Test

Consent to have your blood drawn and tested is usually required, and refusing to take a blood test can have significant consequences, including suspension of driving privileges.

BAC Urine Test

Urine tests are less accurate than breath and blood tests and tend only to be used when other tests are unavailable. Urine testing is considered an intrusive testing method, like blood tests.

Refusing a DUI breath or blood test may help in a DUI criminal case.

Even though a breath/blood test refusal increases your potential DUI penalties, refusing a chemical test could positively impact your *criminal* DUI case.

If you are drunk, prepare to go to jail, do not take the test, just go to jail, continue to refuse the test, and then claim your innocence later at trial, and be found guilty and hit with the maximum penalty. Still, you may win your due to a lack of evidence. Without corroborating DUI chemical test results, the D.A. may not believe the arresting officer is credible. Or they may feel that the officer is not articulate enough to convince a jury of your guilt.

In that event, your DUI charges could be dismissed outright or reduced to wet reckless driving, a less serious charge of reckless driving. Wet reckless driving is sometimes accepted as a plea bargain, admitting to driving with some measurable amount of alcohol in your blood. (Another plea bargain is dry reckless, which means you admit only to driving recklessly with no mention of alcohol.)

The D.A. could dismiss the chemical test refusal charge while leaving the DUI charge in place. If the D.A. is unwilling to reduce or dismiss the charges, one of two things will happen:

You will be allowed to plead guilty or "no contest" to DUI with a chemical test refusal or

You will have to take your case to trial. What happens to your driver's license if you refuse to take a DUI breath or blood test?

The DMV will suspend your license if you refuse to submit a DUI chemical test.

You have ten days from your arrest to request a hearing. Pending the outcome of the hearing, you may postpone your suspension.

Four issues will be addressed at the hearing:

> Did the arresting officer have reason to suspect that you were driving under the influence?
>
> Were you lawfully arrested?
>
> Were you properly advised that your license would be suspended for one year…or revoked for two or three years (with prior DUIs) …if you refused to submit to or failed to complete a DUI chemical test?
>
> Did you willfully refuse to submit to or fail to complete a chemical test after the officer asked you to do so?

The DMV will not suspend your license if you prevail at this hearing. If, however, you are unsuccessful, your punishment will include the following:

A one-year driver's license suspension if it is your first DUI offense,

A two-year license revocation if it is your second DUI offense within ten years or

A three-year license revocation if it is your third DUI offense within ten years.

The DMV will take this action independently of what happens with a criminal or DUI case. However, you may regain your lost driving privileges due to an alleged DUI chemical test refusal if:

You are found not guilty of DUI at trial, or the D.A. dismisses your case due to a lack of evidence.

What happens to your driver's license if you refuse a DUI test and your DUI charges are dismissed? You may be entitled to have a second DMV hearing to try to get your suspension/revocation for a chemical test refusal lifted if, due to a lack of evidence.

The DMV is not required to follow the D.A.'s or the court's lead. The D.A. is concerned with whether there is enough evidence to convict you of a DUI beyond a reasonable doubt.

However, the DMV hearing is an administrative rather than a criminal trial. The DMV needs only to prove that it was *more likely than not* that you improperly refused a DUI chemical test.

What happens to your driver's license if your plea bargains to a "wet reckless" charge? A plea of guilt or "no contest" to a wet reckless or lesser offense will not reverse a DMV license suspension/revocation for a DUI chemical test refusal, even if the prosecutor drops the DUI and test refusal charges.

How Can You Fight a California DUI Test Refusal Charge? Your lawyer should discuss the best defenses with you. Some common defenses in DUI chemical test refusal cases include the following: Your DUI arrest is unlawful if the officer did not have probable cause for a DUI stop or arrest.

The Booking

Once the arrest and official BAC testing are completed and the results show a BAC level of .08% or greater, you are booked into jail for drunk driving. The officer records your information, name, address, age, and physical characteristics during the booking process. The officer then files a report of the alleged crime of drunk driving and any other charges against you.

ORDERS to STAND BACK

Citizens have taken to recording the police's actions. However, when approaching the scene of an investigation or an accident, the police will order everyone back. Do not get involved in an intense negotiation to determine the appropriate distance depending on the circumstances. If you feel your distance from the scene is reasonable, say, "Officer, I have a right to be here. I am filming and not interfering with your work."

Do not argue; decide how far back to stand to avoid arrest. Moving back may end the conflict and still allow you the opportunity to continue.

Do Not Share Your Video with the Police!

Capturing videos of police misconduct or brutality, anonymously upload them to YouTube or live stream on Facebook. Give law enforcement a copy of your recording to ensure every interested party knows all the evidence that may influence their behavior.

Prepare to be arrested for recording officers:

When you go to court, and the arresting officers claim you refused to leave when ordered, the judge may acquit you when your confiscated video proves otherwise.

"Shut it off, or I will arrest you."

At this point, you risk being arrested for testing the boundaries of free speech. So, if the police say they will arrest you, they will. Comply by saying something like, "Okay, Officer. Change your position and move to another spot.

If you keep recording, brace yourself for arrest. Try not to drop your camera, but do not physically resist. As with any arrest, remain silent until you speak with a lawyer.

Remember, the camera might still be recording, so keep calm.

Recording

The First Circuit Court of Appeals (in Boston, Massachusetts) unanimously ruled that citizens had a "constitutionally protected right to videotape police carrying out their duties in public." The law in 38 states allows citizens to record police without physically interfering with the officer's duties.

Twelve states require all parties consent to record any conversation, including California, Massachusetts, Michigan, Montana, Nevada, New Hampshire, Pennsylvania, and Washington. However, in these states, it is technically legal to record on-duty police openly.

Cameras have the potential to be a win-win, helping protect the public against police misconduct and, at the same time, helping protect police against false accusations of abuse.

Departments have supported the installation of video cameras on police car dashboards, in prisons, and during interrogations. At the same time, body cameras can potentially invade the privacy of officers and citizens.

When a police officer is assigned to wear a body, and the camera fails to record or otherwise interferes with camera video, there should be three responses: Direct disciplinary action.

The adoption of rebuttable evidentiary presumptions in favor of the defendant who claims exculpatory evidence was not captured or was destroyed. In other words, they must take the suspect's word.

The adoption (acceptance) of rebuttable evidentiary presumptions on behalf of civil plaintiffs suing the government, police department, and officers for damages based on police misconduct. The presumptions should be rebuttable by other, contrary evidence or proof of challenging circumstances that made compliance impossible. In other words, the officer has proof they had to act in the manner they did instead of following the proper procedure.

Many departments have programs and procedures for using dash cameras. They use digital technology, wirelessly uploading videos and accompanying audio recordings. They do not need to handle videotapes physically, maintaining a secure chain of evidence if used in a legal proceeding.

There are three ways an officer can activate a camera:

> Flipping on the overhead lights automatically starts the camera.
>
> Turning the camera on manually inside the car or
>
> I am activating a wireless microphone.

Some states require officers to notify citizens that their voices are being recorded.

Once in the encounter, decide whether to record the incident. Suppose your record, even if the officer has a body camera. It would help if you did not trust the officer or a third party to record the encounter.

To judge the officer's attitude, ask or inform them you are recording the encounter.

Use of Recordings

The American Civil Liberty Union (ACLU) supports using body cams for police accountability and oversight. They stated this technology should not become a backdoor for any systematic surveillance or tracking of the public. Recordings should be allowed in internal and external investigations of misconduct, and where the police have reasonable suspicion, a recording contains evidence of a crime.

Subject Access

A person recorded by police cams should have access to and the right to make copies of those recordings for however long the government holds them. It should apply to disclosure to a third party if the subject consents or to criminal defense lawyers seeking relevant evidence.

Public Disclosure

For incident recordings to be effective, the public should have access to all police cam videos. Public disclosure of government records can pit two important values against each other: the need for government oversight and the need for transparency. Policymakers must carefully balance these values.

Public disclosure of any recording should be allowed with the subjects' consent.

Redaction of video recordings should be used when it is feasible to blur or black out portions of the video and distort the audio to obscure the identity of subjects.
If recordings are redacted, they should be disclosable. Un-redacted, un-flagged recordings should not be publicly disclosed without the subject's consent.

These recordings do not contain police misconduct or evidence of a crime, so their public oversight value is low. Flagged recordings are those with the highest likelihood of misconduct and where public oversight is needed. Redaction of disclosed recordings is preferred, but unredacted flagged recordings should be publicly disclosable when not feasible because the need for oversight outweighs the privacy interests at stake.

Domestic Disturbance

A domestic disturbance call or situation is a dangerous situation for the officer and the public. Usually, two officers are dispatched to intervene in the disturbance. Officers do not mediate these situations; their job is to separate and maintain a safe environment for all involved.

When officers arrive at a domestic call, they search for the person who made the call, usually a witness, neighbor, or person at the disturbance's residence.

If the officer observes any signs of violence or injury, the suspected person causing the injury will go to jail. Many departments mandate their officers not to attempt to mediate the incident but treat it as a crime.

You are going to jail if you cause an injury, even in self-defense. If you know the police are coming, you go outside and wait to speak with them. Stay calm and cooperative. Avoid any contact with the other person. You do not want a flare-up of the incident in front of the police.

If you are the victim or the accused, video or record as much of the incident as possible to provide evidence on your behalf.

WARRANTS

Suppose an officer suspects a crime has been committed and observes a person walking down the street, and the person matches the suspect's description. The officer will want to search for them and their property. During this incident, the officer does not need an arrest warrant but may need a search warrant.

Privacy laws about obtaining a search warrant differ from those of an arrest warrant. Police may obtain a search warrant by convincing a neutral magistrate or judge that "probable cause" exists to believe criminal activity or evidence of activity occurring in the place to be searched. Usually, the police provide the judge or magistrate with information in written statements under oath, called "affidavits," which report either their observations or those of private citizens or police informants. If the judge believes the affidavit establishes probable cause to search, they will issue a warrant.

The suspect is not present when the warrant is issued and cannot contest the issue of probable cause; the suspect can later challenge the warrant's validity.

The police can only search the place described in a warrant and only the property the warrant describes. If the officer comes across contraband or evidence of a crime not listed on the warrant during their search, they can often seize it.

If the warrant specifies a particular person to be searched, the police can search only that person unless they have independent probable cause to search other individuals who happen to be present at the scene; they can only detain and question the onlooker and, if necessary for their safety, conduct a frisk for weapons (but not a full search).

Many searches occur without warrants. Courts have defined some situations where a search warrant is unnecessary, either because the search was reasonable or because the Fourth Amendment does not apply to all situations due to a lack of a reasonable expectation of privacy.

When getting a warrant, the Fourth Amendment means that no search of an individual may be conducted unless the officer has real and actual belief evidence in each place. With this belief, the officer then makes a sworn statement to a judge, and they will likely find evidence in each place. This belief and oath must be based on evidence given to the officer from statements made by others or physical evidence the officer has obtained. To simplify the Fourth Amendment, the officer must state, "I saw or was told" what they believed to be evidence of a crime.

Believing in the Amendment, people say, "You cannot do this; you cannot search me!" We make statements like the above, believing the officer has no reason or right to suspect us of any crime. However, the word suspicion is just a thought, a feeling, and may not always be based on reality, so in some cases, they can search you, so "stop talking and listen!" Knowing your rights will help you to challenge the officer's reason for the search.

An arrest warrant is an order granted by a judge in a court of law to a law enforcement official granting the officer the right to arrest a person of interest in a crime. Once an officer has an arrest warrant or any other warrant, they have greater police powers than before obtaining the warrant. You must understand your rights are now restricted once the warrant is issued.

The officer presents any relevant evidence to the judge when requesting an arrest warrant, which is why officers or prosecutors ensure they have probable cause and at least two pieces of evidence to present before requesting an arrest warrant.

Arrest warrants require that a crime be committed out of the officer's view. If an officer can see the crime committed, an arrest can be made without a warrant.

Once a judge grants the arrest warrant in a court of law, the local law enforcement officials are legally allowed to arrest the person named on the warrant wherever they find the person. You can be arrested at work, in your residence, or anywhere else.

An arrest warrant and a bench warrant are not the same. A judge issues an arrest warrant for the arrest of a person who has committed a crime.

A judge issues a bench warrant for arresting someone because they failed to appear at a required court hearing.

A bench warrant allows law enforcement officials to arrest the suspect at their residence, their place of work, or anywhere else.

When an arrest warrant is issued, the suspect named in the warrant can be arrested at any time. Law enforcement officials do not always serve an arrest warrant right away.

Outstanding arrest warrants are warrants that have yet to be served by law enforcement. Today, hundreds of thousands of outstanding arrests and warrants exist nationwide. Los Angeles alone has one million outstanding arrest warrants. New Orleans has 49,000 outstanding arrest warrants, and Baltimore, Maryland, has 53,000.

An arrest warrant may be issued even though you did not commit a crime. This situation is true because, with the advent of identity theft across the country, thieves steal people's identities without them finding out and then committing serious crimes in their name.

An arrest warrant can be issued once the crime is committed and the suspect is identified. Sometimes, a warrant is issued for the wrong person. The person it is issued for is incorrect; someone else had stolen and used their identity. Be vigilant about your personal information to prevent identity theft and legal problems.

A search warrant is an order signed by a judge that authorizes police officers to search for specific objects or materials at a specific location. For example, a warrant may authorize the search of "the single-dwelling premises at 11359 Going to Jail Avenue" and direct the police to search for and seize "cash, betting slips, record books, and every other means used about placing bets on horses."

Once you are arrested and booked, a detective will often interview or interrogate you. This interview is designed to get you to confess to the crime.

Good ethical interviews start with the P.E.A.C.E method of the interview process. It is Planning (how to deal with the suspect), (developing some form of rapport with the suspect) Explain, (telling the suspect what will happen), Account (letting the suspect tell their story), Closure (telling the suspect how well they are doing or has done) and evaluate, (decide how truthful the suspect was and how many inconsistent statements have been made). This process is to allow the suspect every opportunity to cooperate and prove their innocence.

Interrogations

Should the interviewer feel they are not getting what they expect, they will turn the interview into more of an

The interrogation should not last more than four hours for minors, mentally ill persons, or a person suffering from a severe disease; in this case, the interrogation cannot last more than two hours.

During the interrogation, the officer offers a theory of the crime, sometimes supported by some evidence, sometimes fabricated, with details that the suspect states back to the officer. You understand that the police can legally lie to you for a confession.

One of the favorite techniques is the Reid Technique, a controversial interrogation method used by police officers and investigators. It consists of the following components.

Designed to eliminate improbable suspects,

Develop suspects or leads,

Increase confidence in identifying truthful or guilty suspects through the interview process,

Identify proper interrogational strategies.

This interview asks behavior-provoking" questions to elicit behavior symptoms of truth or deception from the person being interviewed. Like, "John, what do you think should happen to the person who (did)?" or "What do you think should happen to the kind of person that would do something like this (crime)?" "Did you ever think about (doing anything like), even though you may not have gone through with it?" "John, do you think the person who did this should be given a second chance?" "When the investigation is completed, how will it come out on you?"

It is important to stay silent; you may not know the right answer to the questions. Many job interviewers use these forms of questions to gauge your thinking.

How would you answer the following questions? "How would you have done the crime? What would you have done differently?' Do you know anyone who has done something like this?"

If an interrogator is certain that a suspect is guilty of a crime, they will undergo an accusatory process. The officer aims to elicit the truth" and "obtain a court-admissible confession.

The nine steps of the technique are as follows: The positive confrontation: Tell the suspect something like this: "I have in this file the results of our investigation into the [crime]. The results indicate that you are the person who [committed this crime]." Then, wait for the suspect's reaction,

Theme development: This step blames the suspect's actions on someone or circumstances other than themselves. The goal is to determine why the suspect committed the crime rather than whether they did.

Handling denials: Some officers believe many lying suspects attempt to speak their denials, whereas truthful suspects typically do not ask to talk.

Overcoming objections: If a suspect objects to their criminal allegations, interrogators must agree with the suspect and explain what would happen if their objection was false.

Procurement and retention of suspect's attention: If the suspect is acting defensively and focusing on their potential punishment, the interrogators must intensify the theme and use physical gestures, usually hand gestures, to establish a feeling of understanding.

Handling the suspect's passive mood: If the suspect appears defeated and upset, the investigator must continue the theme and simplify it into a couple of sentences.

Presenting an alternative question: The investigator offers two incriminating choices based on the suspect's guilt.

Having the suspect tell various details of the offense: When the suspect admits guilt after the interrogator's alternative question, the interrogator must follow with a statement of reinforcement and open-ended questions about the details of the alleged crime.

Once the officer has gained a confession, the process is not over. The officer must ensure that the confession stands up in court.

Converting a confession to a written confession: The investigator must use a third party to witness the suspect's oral confession and then translate it into a written one.

During interrogations, suspects often make false confessions. There are false confessions offered in the absence of police interrogation. Most voluntary false confessions appear to result from the suspect having a psychological disturbance or psychiatric disorder.

Then there is a compliant false confession, one given in response to police coercion, stress, or pressure to achieve some instrumental benefit, typically either to terminate or escape from an aversive interrogation process, to take advantage of a perceived suggestion or promise of leniency, or to avoid anticipated harsh punishment, an aspect of compliant false confessions is that they are made knowingly: the suspect admits guilt with the knowledge that he is innocent and that what he says is false. Compliant false confessions are typically recanted shortly after the interrogation is over. The confessor's reason for confessing was to stop the interrogation, and afterward, they used the confession to prove how badly they were treated.

Lastly, the most common type of false confession is the Coerced-compliant false confession. Compliant false confessions result from the sequenced influence process through which detectives seek to persuade a suspect that he is indisputably caught and to mitigate his punishment by confessing.

The main reason to only speak to the police with a lawyer is to protect yourself from saying something that puts you in jeopardy or making a false confession. Based on your interrogation and the police feeling they have enough evidence to take you to trial, you will be arraigned.

The Arraignment

Anytime you are booked (taken to jail and placed in a cell) for any charge or violation, you are assigned an Arraignment Date. The arraignment hearing is the first time you and your lawyer appear in court. It can happen within a day or so of being booked or take a few weeks, depending on how backed up the system is with cases in the County where you were arrested.

If you do not have a lawyer before your arrest, get one before answering questions.

Finding a Lawyer

The following information comes from The State Bar of California.

If you are arrested for committing a crime and cannot afford a lawyer, you may qualify for free help from the public defender's office. Look in the telephone book's white pages under your county's listings. What if there is not a public defender in your area? In such cases, a judge would typically appoint a private attorney to represent you free of charge.

Free legal aid agencies. For non-criminal cases, depending on income and the nature of your legal problem, you can get free or low-cost legal help from a legal services program. Check your telephone book, white pages, or the Internet for lawyers in your area.

You have prepaid legal services plans. You belong to a "legal insurance" plan through your employer, labor union, credit union, credit card company, or as an individual. Your plan may cover the legal work you need, just as medical insurance plans to pay certain medical costs. Your premiums entitle you to a certain amount of a lawyer's time or services at a reduced rate.

You can ask your friends, co-workers, and employers about lawyers. Business owners and professionals such as bankers, ministers, doctors, and social workers might also recommend a lawyer.

You could call a local State Bar-certified lawyer referral service. This type of service refers potential clients to attorneys. After interviewing you, the referral service staff will match you with a lawyer experienced in the appropriate area of the law. (There is usually a small charge for the initial consultation with a lawyer.) For an online list of certified lawyer referral services, visit the State Bar's website, (Keep in mind the service's State Bar certification number must appear in all advertising.)

State Bar-Certified Lawyer Referral Services must meet minimum standards established by the State. The State Bar enforces those standards, and you could turn to the State Bar if you have a problem with the service.

The service can refer you to a lawyer with experience in the field of law relating to your case. It may screen your call to determine whether you have a legal problem or need some other type of assistance. If you need another type of assistance, the referral service can refer you to government agencies or other organizations that are better suited. For example, you might have a problem that could be handled, without charge, by a rent control board or community mediation program or provide you with a bilingual attorney.

Public interest groups. Nonprofit public interest organizations, such as groups concerned with civil liberties and housing discrimination, may help you. Such groups sometimes have staff lawyers who handle such cases. Others provide legal help solely to groups of people rather than to individuals. For example, they might help you and your neighbors convince your city council to install a traffic light at a busy intersection.

Client-attorney matching services where you would typically post a brief case description on the service's website to find an attorney through such a service. Attorney members of the service could then bid on the case by offering you a consultation. The selection of an attorney would be up to you. Such services (bulletin boards) are not State Bar certified lawyer referral services.

Further information not from the Bar Association: If you are arrested and booked into the system, you may need the service of a bail bondsperson. After you have obtained the bondsman's services, you may ask for a list or recommendation of a lawyer specializing in your crime.

At the hearing, the Judge reviews the charges against you and asks you or your lawyer how you plead "guilty," "not guilty," or "no contest."

The Judge issues a future court date. Even though your lawyer is going, and they say you do not need to be present at the arraignment hearing, if you can attend, go. Be fully briefed on what will happen versus relying on second-hand information from your lawyer.

The Plea Bargain

Only take a plea if you are guilty. In the plea bargain, be present with your attorney and the DA at this meeting to agree on the plea you may enter. The DA or your lawyer will attempt to get you not to attend. In this meeting, you must have a skilled attorney to get the best deal possible to avoid going to trial. Most criminal cases are plea-bargained, and many innocent individuals go to prison because of the plea they make.

Delays

Once you have gotten to know the clerk, ask for as many continuances as possible (delays of your trial). Do not lie; plead for a continuance to delay your trial date if possible. The farther you are out of the officer's memory, the better they may forget key facts. Keep in mind that officers make notes about individuals who are not agreeable.

Ask for alternative punishment.

Court clerks often have the authority to let you go to driving school and keep the ticket off your record. Sometimes, you must pay court costs and the ticket, but at least your insurance premiums may not go up, which depends on the court.

Understand your trial and your rights.

If you get a ticket, you are accused of a crime. The ticketing officer signed a sheet of paper swearing you broke a certain traffic law, and he saw you do it.

A sworn statement is called an affidavit, and tickets say that at the top. It is a misdemeanor; it will cost you money, but hopefully, nothing else.

Whatever you do, arrive at your first hearing promptly and dress decently. If you want to know what to wear, go to the court ahead of time to see what best blends in.

You are asked, "What do you plead." Pleading not guilty is a safe bet, although other pleas (e.g., nolo contendre) have strange consequences in court. In some courts, a plea of nolo contendre has the strange effect of making your ticket disappear from the court's files. However, you would want to talk to a local lawyer about that. Politely say, "I plead not guilty, your honor." Do not miss this hearing out of fear, or you will be found guilty. For instance, if the officer does not show up, you are automatically out of the ticket for any reason. (It can happen, no guarantees), talk to the officer or prosecutor before trial and cut a deal. If the officer is nervous about his case against you, he might let you off.

The prosecution presents its case against you. You can respond and call witnesses, and the prosecution can rebut you.

The judge rules whether you are guilty or not guilty. Either take it or appeal it to the court of appeals. Rarely would it be financially wise to appeal a traffic decision, but it is up to you. Moreover, you do have the right.

Unlawful Arrest

Unlawful or false arrest is a common-law tort (a violation leading to civil legal liability) in which a plaintiff alleges they were held in custody without probable cause or an order issued by a court of competent jurisdiction. Stated, "You did nothing," and the officer knew or should have known you did nothing.

With an unlawful arrest, the officer will do as much as possible to get you to confess to avoid scrutinizing your actions in making the arrest.

To be a victim of an unlawful arrest, the arresting person must act with legal authority to make an arrest. Although it is possible to sue law enforcement officials for false arrests, the usual defendants in such cases are private security firms.

Any officer giving false evidence or statements may be guilty of Malicious Prosecution. It is wise that when you find yourself in a situation you feel unlawful on the officer's part, do not physically resist.

Self-defense (physical resistance) to an unlawful arrest or attack by a law enforcement officer is possible but not advised. In Indiana, a law allows people to defend themselves from an unlawful arrest or attack by law enforcement. In other cases, a citizen may be justified in physically defending themselves.

The following cases are included only for those individuals who, for some unbelievable reason, decided to fight the police and lived to go to court.

The following cases are examples of a citizen's right to fight back (but physically fighting or fighting an officer is not advised.)

Some laws state the following: "Citizens may resist unlawful arrest to the point of taking an arresting officer's life if necessary." Plummer v. State, 136 Ind. 306. The United States Supreme Court upheld this premise in John Bad Elk v. U.S., 177 U.S. 529. The Court stated: "Where the officer is killed during the disorder which naturally accompanies an attempted arrest is resisted, the law looks with very different eyes upon the transaction, when the officer had the right to make the arrest, from what it does if the officer had no right. What may be murder in the first case might be nothing more than manslaughter in the other, or the facts might show no offense was committed."

"An arrest made with a defective warrant, one issued without affidavit, or one fails to allege a crime is within the jurisdiction, and the person arrested may resist the arrest and break away. If the arresting officer is killed by one so resisting, the killing may be no more than involuntary manslaughter." Housh v. People, 75 111. 491; reaffirmed and quoted in State v. Leach, 7 Conn. 452; State v. Gleason, 32 Kan. 245; Ballard v. State, 43 Ohio 349; State v Rousseau, 241 P. 2d 447; State v. Spaulding, 34 Minn. 3621.

"When a person, being without fault, is in a place where he has a right to be, is violently assaulted, he may without retreating, repel by force, and if, in the reasonable exercise of his right of self-defense, his assailant is killed, he is justified." Runyan v. State, 57 Ind. 80; Miller v. State, 74 Ind. 1.

"These principles apply to an officer attempting to make an arrest, who abuses his authority and transcends the bounds thereof by the use of unnecessary force and violence, as they do to a private individual unlawfully uses such force and violence." Jones v. State, 26 Tex. App. I; Beaverts v. State, 4 Tex. App. 1 75; Skidmore v. State, 43 Tex. 93, 903.

"One may come to the aid of another person unlawfully arrested, just as you may when a person is assaulted, molested, raped, or kidnapped. Thus, it is not an offense to liberate one from the unlawful custody of an officer, even though he may have submitted to such custody, without resistance." (Adams v. State, 121 Ga. 16, 48 S.E. 910).

With these laws, they seem, and you have rights. However, it would be best to consider that you may fight back but not live to enjoy being right. Be aware of what the officer is saying, especially if you verbally resist an officer/ An officer says in a loud tone something you know is not true, like, "Show me your hands," but your hands are in the air, above your head; the officer's statement means you are in grave danger. If the officer repeats this phrase, you are in danger; the officer's words are inconsistent with the facts. Now, go to the ground as you state as loud as possible, "My hands are in the air. I am not resisting; I am getting on the ground." Say, "I am following your instruction; do not shoot." The officer's words are his defense and are done for the recording of their dashboard camera or body camera. You are in a situation where the officer knows their next actions are not just or within policy.

RULES OF EVIDENCE

What Happens When a Search Violates the Fourth Amendment or the Exclusionary Rule? If a court finds an unreasonable search occurred, evidence seized cannot be used as evidence against the defendant in criminal prosecution. This principle, established by the Supreme Court in 1961, has come to be known as the exclusionary rule.

Many criticize the exclusionary rule, believing it is unfair and "lets the criminals go free because the officer has erred." However, the rule supporters argue that excluding illegally seized evidence is necessary to deter police from conducting illegal searches. Per this argument, the police are less likely to carry out improper searches if the resulting evidence cannot be used to convict the defendant. (There are exceptions to the exclusionary rule.) The exclusionary rule is important to understand what they can and cannot do; this information may get evidence against you thrown out of court.

"Fruit of the poisonous tree doctrine." Not only is the evidence the product of an illegal search inadmissible in court but additional evidence is also derived from the initial evidence. This principle is the "fruit of the poisonous tree" doctrine. If evidence was obtained from an unlawful search, all evidence from the search cannot be used. This fact pertains to evidence gained from future information, like documents.

The "tree" is the evidence the police illegally seized; the "fruit" is the second-generation product of the illegally seized evidence. Both tree and fruit are typically inadmissible at trial.

Some defendants believe the case must be dismissed if they can show a search was illegal. This is not true. The case can continue if a prosecutor has enough other evidence to prove the defendant guilty. The illegally seized evidence can be considered by a judge deciding on an appropriate sentence following conviction and admitted in civil and deportation cases. In some circumstances, a prosecutor can use such evidence to impeach (attack the credibility of) a defendant who testifies at trial.

CORRUPTION

Misconduct and Police Corruption are not the same. Corruption is the abuse of authority for personal gain. It may involve profit or another material benefit obtained illegally from the officer's authority. It is hard for citizens to have corruption investigated.

Corruption includes Bribery, Extortion, receiving or fencing stolen goods, and selling drugs, which refers to patterns of misconduct within a given department or special unit, especially when offenses are repeated with the acquiescence of superiors or through another ongoing failure to correct them. Corruption committed by police officers is classified as follows:

Corruption of authority: When police officers receive free drinks, meals, and other gratuities for being police officers, whether intentionally or unintentionally, they convey an image of corruption, Extortion, and bribery. Not all officers understand when they step over the line.

When an officer demands or receives payment for criminal offenses, to overlook a crime or a potential future crime. Bribery includes the protection of illegal activities, ticket fixing, altering testimony, destroying evidence, and selling criminal information. Bribery is a common act of corruption.

Theft and burglary are when an officer or department steals from an arrest, crime victim, or corpse. For example, individuals taking drugs for personal use in a drug bust and taking personal objects from a corpse at the scene of a crime is corruption.

Theft can occur within a department. An officer can steal property from the department's evidence room or property room for personal use [citation needed].

Shakedowns: Classified under theft and burglary or stealing items for personal use from a crime scene or an arrest.

"Fixing": undermining criminal prosecutions by withholding evidence or failing to appear at judicial hearings, for bribery, or as a personal favor.

Perjury: Lying to protect other officers or oneself in a court of law or a department investigation.

Criminal activities law enforcement officers engage in themselves.

Internal payoffs: prerogatives and prerequisites of law enforcement, such as shifts and holidays, being bought and sold.

The "frame up": the planting or adding to evidence, especially in drug cases.

Police misconduct and corruption are abuses of police authority. Sometimes used interchangeably, the term misconduct refers to a broad range of criminal and civil violations.

Misconduct is the broadest category. Misconduct is.

The act is procedural when it refers to police who violate department rules and regulations, criminal when it refers to police who violate state and federal laws, and unconstitutional when it refers to police who violate a citizen's civil rights or any combination thereof.

Excessive use of Force, discriminatory arrest, physical or verbal harassment, and selective enforcement of the law are common forms of misconduct.

Safeguards against misconduct exist throughout the law. Police departments establish codes of conduct, train recruits, and investigate and discipline officers. They sometimes cooperate with civilian complaint review boards that provide independent evaluative and remedial advice.

These safeguards are only effective when enforced objectively, starting with believing that the officer may violate the law or procedure.

Protections are found in state law, which permits victims to sue the police for damages in civil actions. Typically, these actions are brought for claims such as excessive force ("police brutality"), false arrest and incarceration, Malicious Prosecution, and Wrongful Death. State actions were brought simultaneously with additional claims for constitutional violations. Should you win a case against a police officer, the city will pay the judgment, not the officer or their department. Most of us do not understand that police officers pay the claims for bad police officers' wrongful behavior. No officer can pay a judgment of multi-millions of dollars. Taxes payers will pay these millions even if one officer repeatedly causes lawsuits.

Through both criminal and civil statutes, federal law specifically targets police misconduct. Federal law applies to all state, county, and local officers, including those who work in correctional facilities.

Federal law prohibits discrimination in police work. Any police department receiving federal funding is covered by Title VI of the Civil Rights Act of 1964 (42 U.S.C. § 2000d) and the Office of Justice Programs statute (42 U.S.C. §

3789d[c]), which prohibit discrimination based on race, color, national origin, sex, and religion.

These laws prohibit conduct ranging from racial slurs and unjustified arrests to the refusal of departments to respond to discrimination complaints.

Neither the federal statute nor the civil misconduct provision provides for individual lawsuits. Only the federal government may sue under these laws.

Enforcement is the responsibility of the Justice Department, and convictions are punishable by fines and imprisonment. Civil convictions are remedied through "injunctive relief," a court order requiring a behavior change; typically, resolutions in such cases force police departments to stop abusive practices, institute reform, or submit to court supervision. These rulings rarely benefit the individual.

The individual will not receive any form of physical relief if the case is ruled in their favor.

Plaintiffs must prove willful or unlawful conduct of police; showing mere Negligence or another failure of due care by police officers often does not suffice in court.

Being stupid is not a crime for law enforcement!

In theory, the defense allows police to do their job without fear of Reprisal. In practice, it is increasingly difficult for individuals to sue law enforcement for damages for allegedly violating their civil rights.

COMPLAINTS

If you must file a complaint against an officer, do so promptly. File the report in the same jurisdiction as where the incident took place. You can obtain forms and file a report online. Many police agencies take advantage of the Internet and post forms online. Some agencies allow you to submit online police reports if there are no injuries or if the damage or theft is less than a certain dollar amount.

If the police report involves a motor vehicle, have your driver's license, proof of insurance, and the registration and make copies of these documents for the court.

For incidents involving property theft or damage to property, have the serial numbers and purchase receipts in handy, along with the necessary insurance information.

Police officers ask for identification, phone number, and insurance. Bring proper identification and provide telephone numbers where you can be reached.

To file a police report, you must be eighteen or older; anyone younger must be accompanied by a parent or guardian who agrees to take responsibility for the report.

Do not delay reporting an incident to the police. It is important to visit the police department's website. On the website, citizens can find forms that can be filled out, faxed, or mailed.

Many police departments have a special hotline to report police misconduct. Jurisdictions set a time limit between when the misconduct occurred and when it must be reported.

If you miss the timeline, you may be unable to file a complaint.

A citizen complaint should be made against an officer to receive an immediate investigation. The complaint must charge the officer with a criminal act. If the complaint was filed with a department other than the officer's department, it is filed with the Feds.

A supervisor usually investigates citizen complaints. A complaint is submitted for an investigation and sent to the department's Internal Affairs section. An officer is disciplined or terminated for misconduct by making an internal complaint. They have rights of appeal and will usually get their job back.

The complaint usually stays on the police officer's permanent record even if discipline or termination is not recommended.

Officers who receive many complaints may warrant further investigation. Report misconduct, even if it does not immediately result in disciplinary action or termination.

Citizens unsatisfied with the results of an internal complaint investigation may have the option of filing a criminal complaint against the police officer, beginning a civil lawsuit, or reporting it to another political body like the mayor's office.

While harder than sending a letter, visiting your congressperson's office or their staff, face-to-face is an effective way to influence them. Individuals and groups can arrange personal meetings with Senators and Representatives in their Washington or local offices at various times during the year. To find out when your Senator or Representative will be at their local office, you can call their local office, check their website (House) (Senate), and get on their mailing list.

Making an Appointment

All Congressional offices in Washington require a written appointment request. Some members offer "walk-in" meeting times in their local offices, but an appointment request is still highly recommended.

Appointment requests can be mailed, and faxing may get a faster response. Members' contact information can be found on their websites (House) (and Senate).

Name the others you represent; the more, the merrier. Consider using the following template:

[Your Address] [Date]
The Honorable [full name] U.S. Senate (or U.S. House of Representatives) Washington, DC 20510 (20515 for House)

Dear Senator (or Representative) [last name]:

I am writing to request an appointment with you on [date]. I am a member of the [your group, if any] in [your city], and I am concerned about [issue].

I realize your schedule is difficult to project, but it would be ideal to meet between [time] and [time].

[issue] is important because [1-2 sentences].

My home address is [address]. I can be reached by phone at [phone number] or by email at [email address]. I will contact your office during the week [1-2 weeks before the visit] to confirm the appointment details.

Thank you for considering my request to meet with you.

Sincerely,

Most people have no idea where to file a complaint; here are a few.

• American Civil Liberties Union of the Nation's Capital
www.aclu-nca.org
(202) 457-0800; info@aclu-nca.org

• American Friends Service Committee
www.afsc.org/office/washington-dc
1822 R St., NW, First Floor
(202) 544-0324; localdc@afsc.org

• Covenant House Washington
www.covenanthousedc.org
2001 Mississippi Ave., SE
(202) 610-9600

• D.C. Anti-Violence Project
www.dcavp.org
2000 14th St., NW, Suite 105

(202) 682-2245; info@glovdc.org

• Greater Washington Urban League
www.gwul.org
2901 14th St., NW
(202) 265-8200

• Office on Asian Pacific and Islander Affairs
www.apia.dc.gov
441 4th St., NW, Suite 721 North
(202) 727-3120; oapia@dc.gov

• Office of Gay, Lesbian, Bisexual, and Transgender Affairs
www.glbt.dc.gov
2000 14th St., NW, Second Floor
(202) 727-9493; glbt@dc.gov

• Office on Human Rights
www.ohr.dc.gov
441 4th St., NW, Suite 570N
(202) 727-4559; ohr@dc.gov

•Washington Legal Clinic for the Homeless
www.legalclinic.org
1200 U St., NW 202) 328-5500

PRIVATE SECURITY

The Fourth Amendment does not apply to searches by non-governmental employees (like private security guards) who are not acting on the government's behalf.

For example, assume a shopping mall security guard is acting on a pure hunch search for a teenager's backpack. Inside the backpack, the guard finds a baggie containing an illegal drug.

The guard can detain the teenager, call the police, and turn the drug over to a police officer. The drug is admissible in evidence because the search was conducted by a private security guard acting on his own rather than at the officer's direction.

School systems use private and law enforcement officers to patrol their schools. These systems are different from those of the rest of society.

Under the Constitution of the United States, children under eighteen may have rights just like adults. They should not be "pressured" into answering any question they do not want to answer! Say you will not answer until you have a lawyer or parent present.

Public school students have the First Amendment right to organize politically by passing out leaflets, publishing independent newspapers, putting up posters, etc., just so long as those activities do not disrupt classes or promote drug use. Students can be suspended or expelled if they violate the law or disrupt school activities.

They have the right to a hearing, with their parents or a lawyer present, before being suspended or expelled. Students can have their backpacks and lockers searched by school officials if they have "reasonable suspicion" they are involved in criminal activity, carrying drugs or weapons.

They should not consent to the police or school officials searching their property but should not physically resist, or they may face criminal charges.

Students can be stopped and questioned by school officials without reasonable suspicion, but not for reasons that harass or are discriminatory. If not in class, they can be stopped and questioned about where they are going and why. However, they should not be stopped or questioned for engaging in a legally protected political activity, ethnicity, or religion.

CONCLUSION

Researching and understanding your rights and knowing what an officer can and cannot do should give you a sense of calm when encountering law enforcement. Knowledge is power, and the power to control yourself goes a long way in controlling others. However, dealing with people who feel they are in a war and those they met is untrustworthy and does not need mercy. In this situation, you may do everything right, doing as much as possible to survive a hateful person, but you are still harmed for no reason.

www.ingramcontent.com/pod-product-compliance
Lightning Source LLC
Chambersburg PA
CBHW060356190526
45169CB00002B/630